50 Flavorful Sauces and Marinades

By: Kelly Johnson

Table of Contents

- Classic BBQ Sauce
- Teriyaki Sauce
- Lemon Garlic Marinade
- Honey Mustard Sauce
- Chimichurri Sauce
- Balsamic Glaze
- Soy Ginger Marinade
- Spicy Sriracha Mayo
- Buffalo Sauce
- Sweet Chili Sauce
- Pesto Sauce
- Garlic Butter Sauce
- Peanut Sauce
- Caesar Dressing
- Tzatziki Sauce
- Salsa Verde
- Miso Marinade
- Vinegar and Olive Oil Dressing
- Tomato Basil Sauce
- Hoisin Sauce
- Red Wine Sauce
- Mustard Vinaigrette
- Coconut Curry Sauce
- Lemon Herb Marinade
- Green Goddess Dressing
- Maple Dijon Sauce
- Curry Yogurt Sauce
- Roasted Red Pepper Sauce
- Yogurt and Cucumber Sauce
- Greek Salad Dressing
- Mango Habanero Sauce
- Gochujang Sauce
- Peanut Butter Marinade
- Roasted Garlic Marinade
- Tamarind Sauce

- Blue Cheese Dressing
- Avocado Salsa
- Spicy Chipotle Sauce
- Brown Sugar Bourbon Sauce
- Mint Yogurt Sauce
- Sweet and Sour Sauce
- Creamy Garlic Parmesan Sauce
- Spicy Korean BBQ Sauce
- Lemon Butter Sauce
- Dijon Shallot Vinaigrette
- Tahini Sauce
- Red Pepper Flake Marinade
- Cilantro Lime Sauce
- Pomegranate Molasses Marinade
- Olive Tapenade

Classic BBQ Sauce

Ingredients:

- 1 cup ketchup
- 1/4 cup apple cider vinegar
- 1/4 cup brown sugar
- 2 tbsp Worcestershire sauce
- 1 tbsp Dijon mustard
- 1 tbsp lemon juice
- 1 tsp smoked paprika
- 1/2 tsp garlic powder
- 1/2 tsp onion powder
- 1/4 tsp cayenne pepper (optional)
- Salt and pepper, to taste

Instructions:

1. **Combine Ingredients:** In a saucepan, combine ketchup, apple cider vinegar, brown sugar, Worcestershire sauce, Dijon mustard, lemon juice, smoked paprika, garlic powder, onion powder, and cayenne pepper.
2. **Simmer:** Bring the mixture to a boil over medium heat, then reduce to a simmer. Let it cook for 15-20 minutes, stirring occasionally, until the sauce thickens.
3. **Season:** Taste and adjust the seasoning with salt, pepper, or more sugar if desired.
4. **Cool and Serve:** Let the BBQ sauce cool before serving with grilled meats, burgers, or as a dipping sauce.

Teriyaki Sauce

Ingredients:

- 1/2 cup soy sauce
- 1/4 cup mirin (or white wine if unavailable)
- 2 tbsp honey or brown sugar
- 1 tbsp rice vinegar
- 1 garlic clove, minced
- 1 tsp fresh ginger, grated
- 1 tsp sesame oil
- 1 tbsp cornstarch (optional, for thickening)
- 1 tbsp water (optional, for cornstarch slurry)

Instructions:

1. **Combine Ingredients:** In a saucepan, mix together soy sauce, mirin, honey, rice vinegar, garlic, ginger, and sesame oil.
2. **Simmer:** Bring the mixture to a boil over medium heat, then reduce to low and simmer for 5-7 minutes.
3. **Thicken the Sauce (optional):** In a small bowl, mix cornstarch with water to create a slurry. Add the slurry to the sauce and simmer for another 2-3 minutes until thickened.
4. **Cool and Serve:** Remove from heat and let cool slightly before using as a marinade or dipping sauce.

Lemon Garlic Marinade

Ingredients:

- 1/4 cup olive oil
- 1/4 cup lemon juice (freshly squeezed)
- 3 garlic cloves, minced
- 1 tsp dried oregano
- 1 tsp Dijon mustard
- Salt and pepper, to taste
- 1 tbsp fresh parsley, chopped (optional)

Instructions:

1. **Combine Ingredients:** In a bowl, whisk together olive oil, lemon juice, garlic, oregano, Dijon mustard, salt, and pepper.
2. **Marinate:** Pour the marinade over your choice of meat, seafood, or vegetables. Let it marinate for at least 30 minutes, or up to 2 hours for stronger flavor.
3. **Grill or Cook:** Grill or cook the marinated items as desired. Garnish with fresh parsley if desired.

Honey Mustard Sauce

Ingredients:

- 1/4 cup Dijon mustard
- 1/4 cup honey
- 2 tbsp mayonnaise or Greek yogurt
- 1 tbsp lemon juice
- 1/4 tsp garlic powder
- Salt and pepper, to taste

Instructions:

1. **Combine Ingredients:** In a small bowl, whisk together Dijon mustard, honey, mayonnaise (or Greek yogurt), lemon juice, garlic powder, salt, and pepper.
2. **Serve:** Use immediately as a dipping sauce for chicken tenders, fries, or sandwiches, or refrigerate for later use.

Chimichurri Sauce

Ingredients:

- 1 cup fresh parsley, chopped
- 1/2 cup olive oil
- 3 tbsp red wine vinegar
- 3 garlic cloves, minced
- 1 tsp dried oregano
- 1/4 tsp red pepper flakes
- Salt and pepper, to taste

Instructions:

1. **Combine Ingredients:** In a bowl, combine parsley, olive oil, red wine vinegar, garlic, oregano, red pepper flakes, salt, and pepper.
2. **Let it Sit:** Let the chimichurri sauce sit for at least 30 minutes to allow the flavors to meld.
3. **Serve:** Serve as a topping or marinade for grilled meats, particularly steaks and chicken.

Balsamic Glaze

Ingredients:

- 1 cup balsamic vinegar
- 2 tbsp honey or brown sugar

Instructions:

1. **Simmer:** In a small saucepan, combine balsamic vinegar and honey (or brown sugar).
2. **Reduce:** Bring to a simmer over medium heat and cook for 10-15 minutes, stirring occasionally, until the sauce has thickened to a glaze-like consistency.
3. **Cool and Serve:** Let the balsamic glaze cool before drizzling over salads, roasted vegetables, or grilled meats.

Soy Ginger Marinade

Ingredients:

- 1/4 cup soy sauce
- 2 tbsp rice vinegar
- 2 tbsp honey or brown sugar
- 1 tbsp sesame oil
- 2 garlic cloves, minced
- 1 tsp fresh ginger, grated
- 1 tbsp green onions, chopped (optional)

Instructions:

1. **Combine Ingredients:** In a bowl, whisk together soy sauce, rice vinegar, honey, sesame oil, garlic, ginger, and green onions (if using).
2. **Marinate:** Pour the marinade over your choice of meat, poultry, or tofu. Let it marinate for at least 30 minutes or up to 2 hours.
3. **Cook or Grill:** Grill or pan-sear the marinated items and serve.

Spicy Sriracha Mayo

Ingredients:

- 1/2 cup mayonnaise
- 2 tbsp Sriracha sauce
- 1 tbsp lime juice
- 1/2 tsp garlic powder
- Salt and pepper, to taste

Instructions:

1. **Combine Ingredients:** In a small bowl, mix together mayonnaise, Sriracha, lime juice, garlic powder, salt, and pepper.
2. **Serve:** Use as a dipping sauce for fries, chicken wings, or seafood, or as a topping for burgers and sandwiches.

Buffalo Sauce

Ingredients:

- 1/2 cup hot sauce (such as Frank's RedHot)
- 1/2 cup unsalted butter, melted
- 1 tbsp white vinegar
- 1/4 tsp garlic powder
- 1/4 tsp onion powder
- Salt, to taste

Instructions:

1. **Combine Ingredients:** In a saucepan, combine hot sauce, melted butter, vinegar, garlic powder, onion powder, and salt.
2. **Simmer:** Bring to a simmer over medium heat, stirring occasionally, for 5 minutes.
3. **Serve:** Use immediately to coat chicken wings, or refrigerate for later use.

Sweet Chili Sauce

Ingredients:

- 1/2 cup rice vinegar
- 1/4 cup sugar
- 1/4 cup water
- 2 tbsp fish sauce
- 1 tbsp soy sauce
- 1 garlic clove, minced
- 1/2 tsp red pepper flakes
- 1 tsp cornstarch (optional, for thickening)

Instructions:

1. **Combine Ingredients:** In a saucepan, combine rice vinegar, sugar, water, fish sauce, soy sauce, garlic, and red pepper flakes.
2. **Simmer:** Bring the mixture to a simmer over medium heat and cook for 5-7 minutes until the sugar dissolves and the sauce thickens slightly.
3. **Thicken (optional):** If a thicker consistency is desired, dissolve cornstarch in a small amount of water and add it to the sauce. Simmer for an additional 2-3 minutes until thickened.
4. **Serve:** Use as a dipping sauce for spring rolls, grilled chicken, or shrimp.

Pesto Sauce

Ingredients:

- 2 cups fresh basil leaves
- 1/4 cup pine nuts (or walnuts)
- 2 garlic cloves
- 1/2 cup grated Parmesan cheese
- 1/2 cup extra virgin olive oil
- Salt and pepper, to taste
- 1 tbsp lemon juice (optional)

Instructions:

1. **Blend Ingredients:** In a food processor, combine basil, pine nuts, garlic, Parmesan, lemon juice (if using), salt, and pepper. Pulse until finely chopped.
2. **Add Olive Oil:** With the food processor running, slowly drizzle in the olive oil until the pesto reaches your desired consistency.
3. **Serve:** Toss with pasta, drizzle over grilled vegetables, or use as a spread for sandwiches.

Garlic Butter Sauce

Ingredients:

- 1/2 cup unsalted butter
- 3 garlic cloves, minced
- 1 tbsp fresh parsley, chopped
- 1 tbsp lemon juice (optional)
- Salt and pepper, to taste

Instructions:

1. **Melt Butter:** In a saucepan, melt butter over medium heat.
2. **Cook Garlic:** Add the minced garlic and sauté for 1-2 minutes until fragrant and golden.
3. **Season:** Add parsley, lemon juice (if desired), salt, and pepper. Stir well.
4. **Serve:** Drizzle over seafood, pasta, or use as a dipping sauce for bread.

Peanut Sauce

Ingredients:

- 1/2 cup peanut butter
- 3 tbsp soy sauce
- 1 tbsp honey or brown sugar
- 1 tbsp rice vinegar
- 1 tbsp lime juice
- 1-2 tsp Sriracha or chili paste (optional)
- 2-3 tbsp warm water (to thin out the sauce)

Instructions:

1. **Combine Ingredients:** In a bowl, whisk together peanut butter, soy sauce, honey, rice vinegar, lime juice, and Sriracha.
2. **Thin Sauce:** Gradually add warm water, whisking until the sauce reaches your desired consistency.
3. **Serve:** Use as a dipping sauce for spring rolls, grilled chicken, or drizzle over noodles.

Caesar Dressing

Ingredients:

- 1 egg yolk (or 2 tbsp mayonnaise)
- 1 tbsp Dijon mustard
- 1 garlic clove, minced
- 1/4 cup fresh lemon juice
- 1 cup olive oil
- 1/4 cup grated Parmesan cheese
- 1/2 tsp Worcestershire sauce
- Salt and pepper, to taste

Instructions:

1. **Combine Ingredients:** In a bowl, whisk together egg yolk, Dijon mustard, garlic, lemon juice, Worcestershire sauce, salt, and pepper.
2. **Emulsify:** Slowly drizzle in the olive oil while whisking vigorously until the dressing emulsifies and thickens.
3. **Finish:** Stir in grated Parmesan and adjust seasoning if necessary.
4. **Serve:** Toss with Romaine lettuce, croutons, and more Parmesan for a classic Caesar salad.

Tzatziki Sauce

Ingredients:

- 1 cup Greek yogurt
- 1/2 cucumber, finely grated
- 2 garlic cloves, minced
- 1 tbsp fresh dill, chopped
- 1 tbsp lemon juice
- 1 tbsp olive oil
- Salt and pepper, to taste

Instructions:

1. **Combine Ingredients:** In a bowl, mix together Greek yogurt, grated cucumber, garlic, dill, lemon juice, and olive oil.
2. **Season:** Add salt and pepper to taste.
3. **Chill:** Let the tzatziki sauce chill in the refrigerator for at least 30 minutes to allow the flavors to meld.
4. **Serve:** Use as a dip for pita, grilled meats, or as a topping for falafel.

Salsa Verde

Ingredients:

- 1 lb tomatillos, husked and quartered
- 1-2 jalapeño peppers, seeded (optional for heat)
- 1/2 onion, chopped
- 2 garlic cloves
- 1/4 cup cilantro, chopped
- 1 tbsp lime juice
- Salt, to taste

Instructions:

1. **Roast Tomatillos:** Preheat oven to 400°F (200°C). Spread tomatillos, jalapeños, onion, and garlic on a baking sheet. Roast for 15-20 minutes until soft and charred.
2. **Blend Ingredients:** Transfer the roasted ingredients to a blender or food processor, add cilantro, lime juice, and salt. Blend until smooth.
3. **Serve:** Serve as a dip for chips, or with grilled meats, tacos, or quesadillas.

Miso Marinade

Ingredients:

- 3 tbsp white or yellow miso paste
- 2 tbsp soy sauce
- 1 tbsp rice vinegar
- 1 tbsp honey or brown sugar
- 1 tbsp sesame oil
- 1 garlic clove, minced
- 1 tsp fresh ginger, grated
- 1 tbsp water (to thin the marinade)

Instructions:

1. **Combine Ingredients:** In a bowl, whisk together miso paste, soy sauce, rice vinegar, honey, sesame oil, garlic, ginger, and water.
2. **Marinate:** Pour the marinade over chicken, fish, or tofu and let it marinate for at least 30 minutes, or up to overnight.
3. **Cook:** Grill or pan-sear the marinated items and serve.

Vinegar and Olive Oil Dressing

Ingredients:

- 1/4 cup red wine vinegar (or balsamic vinegar)
- 1/2 cup extra virgin olive oil
- 1 tsp Dijon mustard
- 1 tsp honey (optional)
- Salt and pepper, to taste

Instructions:

1. **Combine Ingredients:** In a small bowl or jar, whisk together vinegar, olive oil, Dijon mustard, honey, salt, and pepper.
2. **Serve:** Drizzle over salads, roasted vegetables, or use as a marinade for meats.

Tomato Basil Sauce

Ingredients:

- 1 can (14.5 oz) crushed tomatoes
- 1 tbsp olive oil
- 2 garlic cloves, minced
- 1/4 cup fresh basil, chopped
- 1/4 tsp dried oregano
- 1/2 tsp sugar (optional)
- Salt and pepper, to taste

Instructions:

1. **Sauté Garlic:** In a saucepan, heat olive oil over medium heat. Add minced garlic and sauté for 1-2 minutes until fragrant.
2. **Add Tomatoes:** Stir in crushed tomatoes, basil, oregano, and sugar (if using). Bring to a simmer and cook for 15-20 minutes, stirring occasionally.
3. **Season:** Taste and adjust seasoning with salt, pepper, or more sugar if necessary.
4. **Serve:** Toss with pasta, use as a pizza sauce, or serve with meatballs.

Hoisin Sauce

Ingredients:

- 1/4 cup soy sauce
- 2 tbsp peanut butter or tahini
- 1 tbsp rice vinegar
- 1 tbsp honey or brown sugar
- 1 tbsp sesame oil
- 1 garlic clove, minced
- 1 tsp Chinese five-spice powder
- 1 tsp Sriracha or chili paste (optional)

Instructions:

1. **Combine Ingredients:** In a small saucepan, whisk together soy sauce, peanut butter, rice vinegar, honey, sesame oil, garlic, five-spice powder, and Sriracha (if using).
2. **Cook:** Heat over low to medium heat, whisking constantly until smooth and warmed through.
3. **Serve:** Use as a dipping sauce for dumplings, spring rolls, or drizzle over stir-fried vegetables and meats.

Red Wine Sauce

Ingredients:

- 1 cup red wine
- 1/2 cup beef broth (or vegetable broth)
- 1 tbsp olive oil
- 1 shallot, finely chopped
- 1 garlic clove, minced
- 1 tbsp fresh thyme or rosemary, chopped
- 1 tbsp butter
- Salt and pepper, to taste

Instructions:

1. **Sauté Shallots and Garlic:** In a saucepan, heat olive oil over medium heat. Add shallot and garlic and cook for 2-3 minutes until softened.
2. **Add Wine and Broth:** Pour in red wine and broth. Bring to a simmer and cook for 10-15 minutes until the sauce has reduced by half.
3. **Finish the Sauce:** Stir in butter, thyme, salt, and pepper. Cook for another 2-3 minutes until the sauce thickens.
4. **Serve:** Drizzle over steaks, roasted meats, or vegetables.

Mustard Vinaigrette

Ingredients:

- 3 tbsp Dijon mustard
- 2 tbsp white wine vinegar
- 1 tbsp honey or maple syrup
- 1/2 cup olive oil
- Salt and pepper, to taste

Instructions:

1. **Combine Ingredients:** In a small bowl, whisk together mustard, vinegar, and honey or maple syrup.
2. **Add Olive Oil:** Slowly drizzle in olive oil while whisking until the dressing emulsifies.
3. **Season:** Add salt and pepper to taste.
4. **Serve:** Drizzle over mixed greens, roasted vegetables, or as a marinade for grilled chicken.

Coconut Curry Sauce

Ingredients:

- 1 can (14 oz) coconut milk
- 2 tbsp curry powder
- 1 tbsp soy sauce
- 1 tsp garlic, minced
- 1 tsp ginger, grated
- 1 tbsp lime juice
- 1 tbsp brown sugar
- 1 tbsp olive oil
- Salt and pepper, to taste

Instructions:

1. **Sauté Aromatics:** In a saucepan, heat olive oil over medium heat. Add garlic and ginger and cook for 1-2 minutes until fragrant.
2. **Add Coconut Milk and Seasonings:** Stir in coconut milk, curry powder, soy sauce, lime juice, and brown sugar. Bring to a simmer.
3. **Simmer:** Cook for 10-15 minutes, stirring occasionally, until the sauce thickens and the flavors meld.
4. **Season:** Taste and adjust with salt and pepper.
5. **Serve:** Pour over rice, vegetables, or grilled meats.

Lemon Herb Marinade

Ingredients:

- 1/4 cup olive oil
- 2 tbsp lemon juice
- 2 tbsp fresh parsley, chopped
- 1 tbsp fresh thyme, chopped
- 2 garlic cloves, minced
- Salt and pepper, to taste

Instructions:

1. **Combine Ingredients:** In a bowl, whisk together olive oil, lemon juice, parsley, thyme, garlic, salt, and pepper.
2. **Marinate:** Pour the marinade over chicken, fish, or vegetables and let marinate in the refrigerator for at least 30 minutes to 2 hours.
3. **Cook:** Grill or roast the marinated items and serve.

Green Goddess Dressing

Ingredients:

- 1/2 cup Greek yogurt
- 1/4 cup mayonnaise
- 2 tbsp lemon juice
- 2 tbsp fresh parsley, chopped
- 1 tbsp fresh tarragon, chopped
- 1 tbsp chives, chopped
- 1 garlic clove, minced
- Salt and pepper, to taste

Instructions:

1. **Combine Ingredients:** In a bowl or food processor, combine Greek yogurt, mayonnaise, lemon juice, parsley, tarragon, chives, garlic, salt, and pepper.
2. **Blend:** Whisk or blend until smooth and creamy.
3. **Serve:** Drizzle over salads, roasted vegetables, or use as a dip for crudités.

Maple Dijon Sauce

Ingredients:

- 3 tbsp Dijon mustard
- 2 tbsp maple syrup
- 1 tbsp apple cider vinegar
- 1/4 cup olive oil
- Salt and pepper, to taste

Instructions:

1. **Combine Ingredients:** In a small bowl, whisk together Dijon mustard, maple syrup, and apple cider vinegar.
2. **Add Olive Oil:** Slowly drizzle in olive oil while whisking until smooth.
3. **Season:** Add salt and pepper to taste.
4. **Serve:** Use as a sauce for grilled meats, roasted vegetables, or as a dressing for salads.

Curry Yogurt Sauce

Ingredients:

- 1/2 cup Greek yogurt
- 1 tbsp curry powder
- 1 tbsp lemon juice
- 1 tsp honey or maple syrup
- 1 garlic clove, minced
- Salt and pepper, to taste

Instructions:

1. **Combine Ingredients:** In a bowl, mix Greek yogurt, curry powder, lemon juice, honey, garlic, salt, and pepper.
2. **Blend:** Stir until well combined and smooth.
3. **Serve:** Serve as a dip for veggies, a topping for roasted vegetables, or as a sauce for grilled chicken.

Roasted Red Pepper Sauce

Ingredients:

- 2 red bell peppers, roasted and peeled
- 1/2 cup heavy cream or coconut cream
- 1 tbsp olive oil
- 1 garlic clove, minced
- 1/4 tsp smoked paprika
- Salt and pepper, to taste

Instructions:

1. **Roast Peppers:** Roast the red bell peppers over an open flame or in the oven until charred. Peel off the skins and remove the seeds.
2. **Blend Ingredients:** In a blender, combine roasted peppers, heavy cream, olive oil, garlic, paprika, salt, and pepper. Blend until smooth.
3. **Simmer:** Pour the sauce into a pan and heat over low-medium heat for 5-10 minutes until warm and thickened.
4. **Serve:** Drizzle over pasta, grilled meats, or roasted vegetables.

Yogurt and Cucumber Sauce (Tzatziki)

Ingredients:

- 1 cup Greek yogurt
- 1/2 cucumber, grated and excess water squeezed out
- 1 garlic clove, minced
- 1 tbsp fresh dill, chopped (or mint, if preferred)
- 1 tbsp lemon juice
- 1 tbsp olive oil
- Salt and pepper, to taste

Instructions:

1. **Prepare Cucumber:** Grate the cucumber and squeeze out any excess water using a clean cloth or paper towel.
2. **Combine Ingredients:** In a bowl, mix the yogurt, cucumber, garlic, dill, lemon juice, and olive oil.
3. **Season:** Add salt and pepper to taste.
4. **Serve:** Serve as a dip with pita bread, veggies, or as a sauce for grilled meats and gyros.

Greek Salad Dressing

Ingredients:

- 1/4 cup red wine vinegar
- 1/2 cup olive oil
- 1 tbsp lemon juice
- 1 tsp dried oregano
- 1 garlic clove, minced
- Salt and pepper, to taste

Instructions:

1. **Combine Ingredients:** In a bowl, whisk together red wine vinegar, olive oil, lemon juice, oregano, garlic, salt, and pepper.
2. **Serve:** Drizzle over a Greek salad or use as a marinade for vegetables or chicken.

Mango Habanero Sauce

Ingredients:

- 1 ripe mango, peeled and chopped
- 2 habanero peppers, seeds removed (use gloves)
- 1/4 cup lime juice
- 2 tbsp honey
- 1/4 cup apple cider vinegar
- 1 tbsp olive oil
- Salt, to taste

Instructions:

1. **Blend Ingredients:** In a blender, combine mango, habanero peppers, lime juice, honey, vinegar, olive oil, and salt.
2. **Blend:** Blend until smooth and creamy.
3. **Serve:** Use as a dipping sauce for grilled meats or seafood, or as a glaze for roasted vegetables.

Gochujang Sauce

Ingredients:

- 2 tbsp Gochujang (Korean chili paste)
- 2 tbsp soy sauce
- 1 tbsp sesame oil
- 1 tbsp rice vinegar
- 1 tsp honey or brown sugar
- 1 garlic clove, minced

Instructions:

1. **Combine Ingredients:** In a bowl, whisk together Gochujang, soy sauce, sesame oil, rice vinegar, honey, and garlic.
2. **Serve:** Use as a marinade for meats, a dipping sauce for dumplings, or drizzle over stir-fried vegetables.

Peanut Butter Marinade

Ingredients:

- 1/4 cup peanut butter
- 2 tbsp soy sauce
- 1 tbsp rice vinegar
- 1 tbsp honey or maple syrup
- 1 tsp sesame oil
- 1 garlic clove, minced
- 1 tsp grated fresh ginger

Instructions:

1. **Combine Ingredients:** In a bowl, whisk together peanut butter, soy sauce, rice vinegar, honey, sesame oil, garlic, and ginger.
2. **Marinate:** Use as a marinade for chicken, tofu, or vegetables. Let marinate for at least 30 minutes before cooking.

Roasted Garlic Marinade

Ingredients:

- 1 head of garlic, roasted
- 1/4 cup olive oil
- 1 tbsp balsamic vinegar
- 1 tbsp Dijon mustard
- 1 tsp fresh thyme, chopped
- Salt and pepper, to taste

Instructions:

1. **Roast Garlic:** Slice the top off the garlic head, drizzle with olive oil, and wrap in foil. Roast in the oven at 400°F (200°C) for 30 minutes or until soft.
2. **Combine Ingredients:** Squeeze the roasted garlic out of its skin and combine with olive oil, balsamic vinegar, Dijon mustard, thyme, salt, and pepper.
3. **Marinate:** Use as a marinade for chicken, lamb, or vegetables. Marinate for at least 1 hour.

Tamarind Sauce

Ingredients:

- 2 tbsp tamarind paste
- 1/4 cup water
- 2 tbsp brown sugar
- 1 tbsp soy sauce
- 1/2 tsp ground cumin
- 1/4 tsp ground coriander
- 1 garlic clove, minced
- Salt, to taste

Instructions:

1. **Combine Ingredients:** In a saucepan, whisk together tamarind paste, water, brown sugar, soy sauce, cumin, coriander, and garlic.
2. **Simmer:** Heat the mixture over medium heat for 5-7 minutes, stirring occasionally, until the sauce thickens.
3. **Season:** Add salt to taste.
4. **Serve:** Drizzle over grilled meats, vegetables, or use as a dipping sauce.

Blue Cheese Dressing

Ingredients:

- 1/2 cup mayonnaise
- 1/4 cup sour cream
- 1/2 cup crumbled blue cheese
- 1 tbsp lemon juice
- 1 tbsp white wine vinegar
- 1/2 tsp garlic powder
- Salt and pepper, to taste

Instructions:

1. **Combine Ingredients:** In a bowl, mix mayonnaise, sour cream, crumbled blue cheese, lemon juice, white wine vinegar, and garlic powder.
2. **Blend:** Stir until smooth and well combined. Adjust the consistency with a little water or milk if needed.
3. **Serve:** Drizzle over salads, serve with buffalo wings, or as a dip for vegetables.

Avocado Salsa

Ingredients:

- 2 ripe avocados, peeled and diced
- 1 small red onion, finely chopped
- 1 tomato, diced
- 1/4 cup fresh cilantro, chopped
- 1 jalapeño pepper, deseeded and minced (optional for heat)
- 1 tbsp lime juice
- Salt and pepper, to taste

Instructions:

1. **Combine Ingredients:** In a medium bowl, combine diced avocado, onion, tomato, cilantro, and jalapeño (if using).
2. **Season:** Drizzle with lime juice and season with salt and pepper.
3. **Serve:** Serve as a topping for tacos, grilled meats, or as a dip with tortilla chips.

Spicy Chipotle Sauce

Ingredients:

- 2 chipotle peppers in adobo sauce
- 1/2 cup mayonnaise
- 1 tbsp lime juice
- 1 garlic clove, minced
- 1 tsp smoked paprika
- 1/2 tsp cumin
- Salt and pepper, to taste

Instructions:

1. **Blend Ingredients:** In a blender or food processor, combine chipotle peppers, mayonnaise, lime juice, garlic, smoked paprika, cumin, and a pinch of salt and pepper.
2. **Blend:** Process until smooth and creamy.
3. **Serve:** Use as a sauce for grilled meats, tacos, or as a dip for fries.

Brown Sugar Bourbon Sauce

Ingredients:

- 1/4 cup bourbon
- 1/2 cup brown sugar
- 1/4 cup soy sauce
- 2 tbsp Dijon mustard
- 1 tbsp apple cider vinegar
- 1/2 tsp garlic powder
- 1/2 tsp onion powder
- 1/4 tsp black pepper

Instructions:

1. **Combine Ingredients:** In a saucepan, combine bourbon, brown sugar, soy sauce, Dijon mustard, apple cider vinegar, garlic powder, onion powder, and black pepper.
2. **Simmer:** Heat over medium heat and bring to a simmer. Let cook for 5-7 minutes, stirring occasionally, until it thickens.
3. **Serve:** Use as a glaze for meats such as pork, chicken, or steak.

Mint Yogurt Sauce

Ingredients:

- 1 cup Greek yogurt
- 2 tbsp fresh mint, chopped
- 1 tbsp lemon juice
- 1 tbsp honey
- Salt and pepper, to taste

Instructions:

1. **Combine Ingredients:** In a bowl, mix together Greek yogurt, mint, lemon juice, and honey.
2. **Season:** Add salt and pepper to taste.
3. **Serve:** Serve with lamb, grilled vegetables, or as a dip for pita bread.

Sweet and Sour Sauce

Ingredients:

- 1/2 cup white vinegar
- 1/2 cup ketchup
- 1/4 cup sugar
- 1 tbsp soy sauce
- 1 tbsp cornstarch mixed with 2 tbsp water

Instructions:

1. **Combine Ingredients:** In a saucepan, combine vinegar, ketchup, sugar, and soy sauce.
2. **Simmer:** Bring to a simmer over medium heat, stirring occasionally.
3. **Thicken:** Stir in the cornstarch mixture and cook for an additional 2-3 minutes until the sauce thickens.
4. **Serve:** Serve with fried foods, spring rolls, or as a dipping sauce.

Creamy Garlic Parmesan Sauce

Ingredients:

- 1/2 cup heavy cream
- 1/4 cup grated Parmesan cheese
- 2 garlic cloves, minced
- 2 tbsp butter
- Salt and pepper, to taste
- 1 tbsp fresh parsley, chopped (optional)

Instructions:

1. **Melt Butter:** In a saucepan, melt butter over medium heat and sauté garlic until fragrant (about 1-2 minutes).
2. **Add Cream and Parmesan:** Stir in the heavy cream and bring to a simmer. Once it simmers, add Parmesan cheese and stir until melted and smooth.
3. **Season:** Add salt and pepper to taste.
4. **Serve:** Drizzle over pasta, grilled chicken, or vegetables. Garnish with fresh parsley if desired.

Spicy Korean BBQ Sauce

Ingredients:

- 3 tbsp Gochujang (Korean chili paste)
- 2 tbsp soy sauce
- 2 tbsp rice vinegar
- 1 tbsp honey or brown sugar
- 1 tbsp sesame oil
- 1 garlic clove, minced
- 1 tsp grated fresh ginger
- 1 tsp sesame seeds (optional)

Instructions:

1. **Combine Ingredients:** In a bowl, mix together Gochujang, soy sauce, rice vinegar, honey, sesame oil, garlic, and ginger.
2. **Mix:** Stir until smooth and well combined.
3. **Serve:** Use as a marinade for meats, a dipping sauce for dumplings, or drizzle over grilled vegetables. Garnish with sesame seeds if desired.

Lemon Butter Sauce

Ingredients:

- 1/2 cup unsalted butter
- 2 tbsp fresh lemon juice
- 1 garlic clove, minced
- 1 tsp lemon zest
- Salt and freshly ground black pepper, to taste
- 1 tbsp fresh parsley, chopped (optional)

Instructions:

1. **Melt Butter:** In a saucepan, melt butter over medium heat.
2. **Add Garlic and Lemon:** Stir in the minced garlic and sauté for about 1 minute until fragrant. Add the lemon juice and zest.
3. **Season:** Season with salt and pepper to taste.
4. **Serve:** Drizzle over seafood, grilled chicken, or vegetables. Garnish with chopped parsley if desired.

Dijon Shallot Vinaigrette

Ingredients:

- 2 tbsp Dijon mustard
- 1 small shallot, finely minced
- 3 tbsp white wine vinegar
- 1/4 cup extra virgin olive oil
- 1 tsp honey (optional for sweetness)
- Salt and freshly ground black pepper, to taste

Instructions:

1. **Mix Mustard and Vinegar:** In a small bowl, whisk together Dijon mustard, minced shallot, and white wine vinegar.
2. **Add Olive Oil:** Gradually whisk in the olive oil until the dressing is emulsified.
3. **Season:** Stir in honey (if using) and season with salt and pepper.
4. **Serve:** Use as a dressing for salads, or drizzle over roasted vegetables or grilled meats.

Tahini Sauce

Ingredients:

- 1/2 cup tahini (sesame paste)
- 2 tbsp lemon juice
- 1 garlic clove, minced
- 1/4 cup water (or more to adjust consistency)
- 1 tbsp olive oil
- Salt, to taste
- 1/2 tsp ground cumin (optional)

Instructions:

1. **Combine Ingredients:** In a bowl, whisk together tahini, lemon juice, minced garlic, and olive oil.
2. **Adjust Consistency:** Gradually add water, a little at a time, until you reach a smooth, pourable consistency.
3. **Season:** Stir in salt to taste and optional cumin for added flavor.
4. **Serve:** Serve as a dip for veggies, pita, or drizzle over falafel, roasted vegetables, or bowls.

Red Pepper Flake Marinade

Ingredients:

- 1/4 cup olive oil
- 1 tbsp red pepper flakes
- 2 tbsp red wine vinegar
- 2 garlic cloves, minced
- 1 tsp dried oregano
- Salt and freshly ground black pepper, to taste

Instructions:

1. **Combine Ingredients:** In a bowl, whisk together olive oil, red pepper flakes, red wine vinegar, minced garlic, and oregano.
2. **Season:** Add salt and pepper to taste.
3. **Marinate:** Pour the marinade over meats, tofu, or vegetables. Let it marinate for at least 30 minutes before grilling or roasting for best results.

Cilantro Lime Sauce

Ingredients:

- 1/2 cup fresh cilantro, chopped
- 1/4 cup sour cream or Greek yogurt
- 2 tbsp lime juice
- 1 garlic clove, minced
- 1 tbsp olive oil
- Salt and freshly ground black pepper, to taste

Instructions:

1. **Blend Ingredients:** In a food processor or blender, combine cilantro, sour cream or Greek yogurt, lime juice, garlic, and olive oil.
2. **Season:** Blend until smooth and season with salt and pepper to taste.
3. **Serve:** Drizzle over tacos, grilled chicken, or roasted vegetables.

Pomegranate Molasses Marinade

Ingredients:

- 1/4 cup pomegranate molasses
- 2 tbsp olive oil
- 1 tbsp red wine vinegar
- 1 garlic clove, minced
- 1 tsp ground cumin
- Salt and freshly ground black pepper, to taste

Instructions:

1. **Combine Ingredients:** In a bowl, whisk together pomegranate molasses, olive oil, red wine vinegar, minced garlic, and ground cumin.
2. **Season:** Add salt and pepper to taste.
3. **Marinate:** Use as a marinade for chicken, lamb, or roasted vegetables. Let marinate for at least 30 minutes before cooking.

Olive Tapenade

Ingredients:

- 1 cup pitted Kalamata olives
- 1/4 cup green olives, pitted
- 2 tbsp capers, drained
- 2 garlic cloves, minced
- 2 tbsp extra virgin olive oil
- 1 tbsp fresh lemon juice
- 1 tbsp fresh parsley, chopped

- Salt and freshly ground black pepper, to taste

Instructions:

1. **Combine Ingredients:** In a food processor, combine Kalamata olives, green olives, capers, garlic, olive oil, and lemon juice.
2. **Pulse:** Pulse until the mixture is finely chopped but still chunky.
3. **Season:** Stir in chopped parsley, and season with salt and pepper to taste.
4. **Serve:** Serve as an appetizer with crusty bread, crackers, or use as a topping for grilled meats or vegetables.

www.ingramcontent.com/pod-product-compliance
Lightning Source LLC
LaVergne TN
LVHW081509060526
838201LV00056BA/3012